Fall

In fall, the days grow cool, and sometimes there is frost at night.

Winter

In winter, it is cold most of the time. In many places there is snow.

Ladybird FIRST FACTS ABOUT ™
WEATHER

By Caroline Arnold
Illustrated by Jan Pyk

Ladybird Books

What's the weather today?

Is it hot or cold?
Is the sun shining?

Is it raining?

Is it windy?

Do you see snow?

Changes in the air around us happen all the time.

They are what we call the weather.

The temperature of the air tells us if the weather is hot or cold.

We measure temperature with a thermometer.

Look at the top of the dark line inside a thermometer. The number next to it is the temperature. We measure temperature in degrees (°).

We usually use the Fahrenheit scale to report the temperature.

°F
Fahrenheit

°C
Celsius

110

100

90

80

70

60

50

40

30

20

10

0

-10

40

30

20

10

0

-10

-20

6

People cannot live where it is too hot or too cold.

In the desert, the daytime temperature can be more than 130 degrees.

The coldest temperature ever recorded was more than 100 degrees below zero!

Most people prefer temperatures around 65 degrees.

The earth gets its heat from the sun.

Each morning, the sun warms the earth. The warm earth heats the air above it.

As the day goes by, the air gets hotter and hotter.

When the sun goes down, the earth and air become cooler again.

Warm air is lighter than cold air. When hot air rises, cold air moves in to take its place. Moving air is what we call wind.

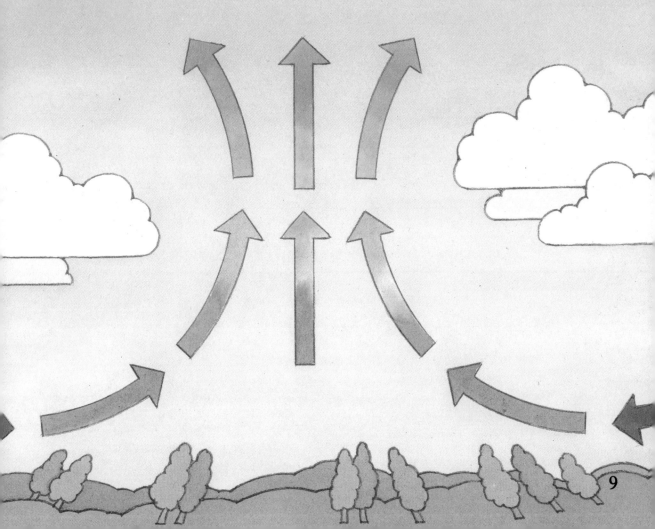

The wind helps us in
many ways.

It brings us fresh air.

It scatters seeds and pollen.

It helps boats sail and airplanes fly.

You can use the wind to fly a kite.

It can turn mills to pump water or to produce electricity.

When the wind blows, the air seems colder than when it is still. Weather forecasters call this the wind chill factor.

We can measure both the direction and speed of the wind.

The arrow of the weather vane points into the wind. This wind is blowing from the east.

A windsock helps pilots know which way to land and take off.

An anemometer tells us how hard the wind is blowing. The stronger the wind, the faster it turns.

A gentle breeze blows at about 10 miles an hour.

A medium gale blows at about 25 miles an hour.

In a storm, the wind blows at up to 72 miles an hour.

Any wind stronger than 72 miles an hour is a hurricane.

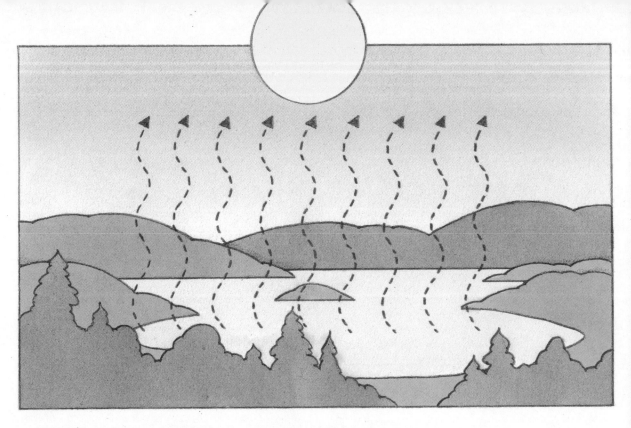

Much of the earth is covered with water.

When the sun warms the water, some of it evaporates into the air. It becomes water vapor.

The amount of water vapor in the air is what we call humidity. When the humidity is high, there is a lot of water in the air, and it seems heavy and sticky.

At night, when the air cools, water vapor collects as drops on the ground. It becomes dew.

If the temperature falls below freezing, the dew becomes frost. In the morning light, frost makes the ground look as if it has been sprinkled with diamonds.

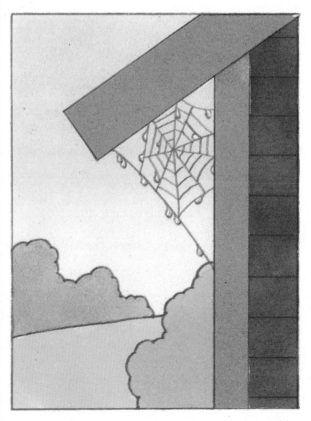 

As water vapor rises with warm air into the sky, it cools off. These tiny drops of water come together to form clouds.

Cumulus clouds are fat and puffy. Usually they mean fair weather.

Stratus clouds form in sheets or layers. Often they bring rain.

High wispy clouds are called cirrus clouds. They are made up of tiny pieces of ice high in the sky.

Low clouds along the ground are called fog.

The water vapor in clouds comes back to earth as rain, sleet, snow, or hail.

Inside a cloud the tiny drops of water bump into one another and create bigger drops. A million tiny droplets are needed to make one raindrop.

When the raindrops grow too heavy to stay in the air, they fall to earth.

Sleet forms when rain falls through freezing air and turns to ice.

Snowflakes form when small crystals of ice grow on tiny bits of dust in the air. All snowflakes have six sides. No two snowflakes are exactly alike.

When rain freezes into a ball of ice it becomes a hailstone. Sometimes hailstones can be as big as baseballs!

19

Some rain is soft and gentle. But sometimes rain comes suddenly, along with lightning and noisy thunder.

When a storm is over, look at the sky. Maybe you will see a rainbow. A rainbow occurs when sunlight shines through raindrops.

Most storms come and go quickly. But sometimes we have huge, terrible storms.

A tornado is a funnel of wind that reaches down to earth from a low cloud. It is so strong that it can suck cars, houses, or animals into the air. Most tornadoes occur in the midwestern United States.

Blizzards are huge snowstorms. Strong winds from blizzards pile snow into giant drifts.

A hurricane is a very large circular storm. It can be hundreds of miles across. A hurricane starts over the ocean. As it moves over land, it brings strong winds and heavy rain. Hurricanes often cause flooding, and their winds can blow down trees and buildings.

Weather reporters warn us about tornadoes, hurricanes, and blizzards so that we can go to a safe place until they are over.

Do you listen to the weather report on radio or television?

The weather report tells us about the weather where we live and in other parts of the world. It also tells us what kind of weather to expect in the next few days.

We learn about the weather in many ways.

Weather stations all over the world record information about temperature, humidity, and wind.

Satellites in space take pictures of the earth's weather.

High above the earth, special weather balloons collect facts about the air.

Computers help us understand weather information.

Everyone wants to know what the weather will be. It helps us plan what to wear and what to do.

Farmers want to know when to plant and harvest their crops.

Pilots want to know if it is safe to fly.

Other people want to know if they can plan a picnic or if they should bring an umbrella to work.

Skiers want to know where there will be snow.

Every day the weather changes.

What's the weather today where you live?

GLOSSARY

anemometer   a device used to measure wind speed

blizzard   a violent snowstorm with strong winds

cirrus clouds   high, wispy clouds

cumulus clouds   puffy, rounded clouds

evaporate   to turn into a vapor or gas

fog   water vapor near the ground

gale   a strong wind

humidity   the amount of moisture in the air

hurricane   a large, circular storm

stratus clouds   flat, sheet-like clouds

temperature   degree of hotness or coldness

thermometer   a device used to measure temperature

tornado   a spinning, funnel-shaped wind

water vapor   water in the form of gas, as in steam

weather vane   a device used to show wind direction

wind chill factor   the amount of cooling caused by the wind

windsock   a cone-shaped tube used to show wind direction